BE CREATIVE!
A STYLING GUIDE
for
Natural Hair Braids
& Dread Locs

D1282616

This book is the property of

_____

Design and Layout by

Mr. Sketch
Graphic Designs & Artwork

JAN HU 20

**Dr. Calisa Cruickshank
seen here wearing
"Cinnamon Rolls"**

To my readers,

I decided to pursue my locs of happiness
September 2008. Since then we have be
happily married. After a lifetime of ir
combs, blow drying, braids and weav
I finally decided to take the big step a
commit to this once "dreadful" hairstyle,
hairstyle that I always admired.

When I first started my locs like any fem
trying something new, I asked family a
friends for their opinions. I told a childhc
friend and she responded by saying " W
do you want locs? She later said "Locs ar
versatile enough, you can only wear th
up or down."

Someone else said "Aren't you studying tc
a doctor ?" , "Why do you want locs ?",
added "That look is unprofessional!"And
but not least a male friend told me "Eww
those things are nasty it reminds me
homeless people." And the list goes on.

Now if you ask anyone who knows me,
will tell you that I am a very strong min
individual, so of course I grew my locs.
made it my business to break the stereot
most often associated with locs and na
hair styles in my own way. I wanted my
to be a hairstyle that's envied, respe
loved and embraced. I hope to dc
by inspiring others with this styling g
to "BE CREATIVE" with their hair
------ Wadada.

Table of Contents

JAN 2019

Side Twist and Side Twist Pin Up

What to do!

- Ok now this style is easy to do and requires little to no time at all. It's best suited for medium to long hair.
- So you want to pull all of your hair to one side.
- Then divide into two sections.
- Now twist these two sections of hair into one big twist and secure the end with a rubber band.
- You can leave you hair like this as a side twist or pin it up.
- Now for the, pin up style, simply take the twist and fold the twisted hair backwards.
- Then secure the ends of the twisted hair to scalp on the same side of the twist with hairpins.

BE CREATIVE *and combine with a Twisted Crown, Swirly Swirl or few Hair Flowers.*

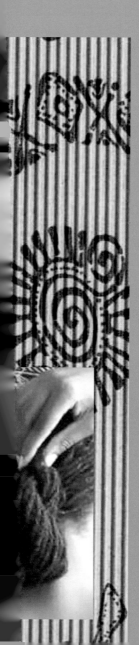

1

2

3

What to do!

- This is one of my favorite styles.
- To start take approximately 6 to 8 locs depending on how large you want to the swirl to be.
- Next secure the end of the locs with a rubber band.
- Then, starting from the tips roll up the bunch of hair in a circular motion. This rolling technique is similar to the way you would roll up a tape measure.
- Your hair should look like a "flat coil".
- Secure with hairpins.

BE CREATIVE *and combine with a Side Braid, Side Twist, Sweet Bun or even a simple ponytail.*

4

5

Side Braid and Side Braid Pin Up

1

2

3

4

4

What to do!

- This is another great style for medium to long hair
- Start with pulling all your hair to one side.
- Then divide into three sections.
- Now braid from scalp to tip crossing one section over the other.
- There will be some unevenness, especially if you have locs, but it does not mean that you did not do it right. It is expected and easy to fix.
- Simply secure ends with rubber bands and use hair pins to secure those loose ends that may be sticking out.
- This a great tension free hairstyle that can give your hair a "styling break".
- This particular style is versatile, meaning that it can be converted into a pin up style.
- Simply take the end of the braid and fold backwards. Now tuck the tip of the braid under a small section of hair to give that neat appearance.

BE CREATIVE *and combine with Braided Crown, Twisted Bangs or Flower Crown.*

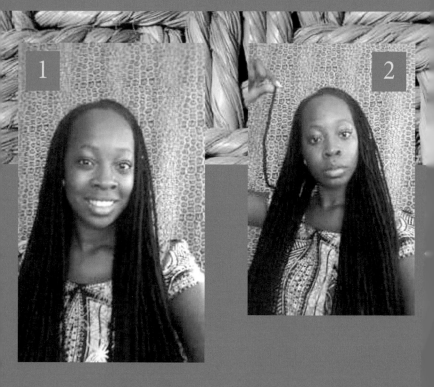

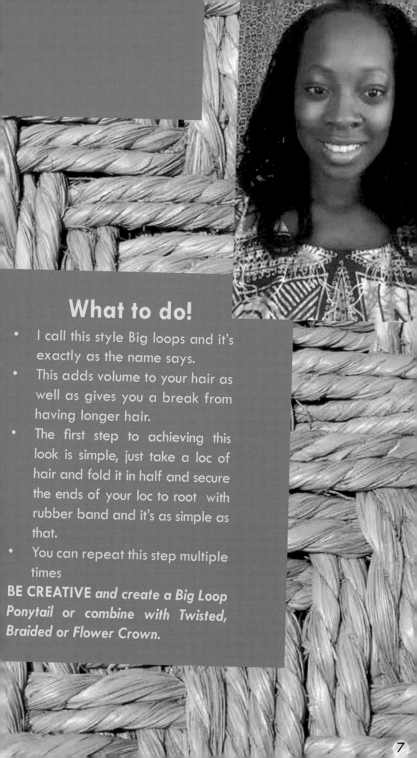

What to do!

- I call this style Big loops and it's exactly as the name says.
- This adds volume to your hair as well as gives you a break from having longer hair.
- The first step to achieving this look is simple, just take a loc of hair and fold it in half and secure the ends of your loc to root with rubber band and it's as simple as that.
- You can repeat this step multiple times

BE CREATIVE *and create a Big Loop Ponytail or combine with Twisted, Braided or Flower Crown.*

TWISTED BANGS

What to do!

- Try these Twisted Bangs.
- Take a few locs of hair from the top of the head.
- Simply fold in half or quarter (now how much you fold will determine the length of the bangs).
- After folding the hair, twist the ends in a clockwise direction.
- Now drape the hair over the crown of your head.
- Then secure the ends with a hair pin.
- And it's as simple as that.

BE CREATIVE *and combine with a Sweet Bun, Side Braid or Side Twist Pin Up style.*

Hair Butterflies

What to do!

- Try out this youthful style.
- The size of your butterfly depends on you.
- To start take one loc of hair and fold it making a loop. (Now the size of the loop will determine the size of the butterfly.)
- Secure the end of the loc to the shaft of the loc with a rubber band.
- Now fold that same loop into half and secure with rubber band creating two smaller loops, that should resemble an infinity sign.
- Then take each loop and fold in half again securing with a rubber band each time.
- When you're done there should be four small loops.
- You can create one butterfly or as many as you like.

BE CREATIVE *and use mutli-coloured rubber bands or beads placed close to the end of the loc and midway along the shaft of the loc. You can also combine Hair Butterflies with Hair Flowers.*

1

2

3

4

What to do!

- This is another fun style for the younger age group.
- It's very easy and you will be amazed at how creative you will feel when you're done.
- To begin take a loc of hair starting at the end make one small loop and secure with a rubber band.
- Make four more loops along the loc ensuring that each loop is close together.
- The size of the loop depends on your preference.
- After you have a total of five loops take the first loop and attach to the last loop by securing with a rubber band.
- This can be worn with varying lengths and sizes of flowers.

BE CREATIVE *and combine with a Sweet Bun, Twisted Pony Tail or Hair Butterflies.*

Loc Knots with Curlies

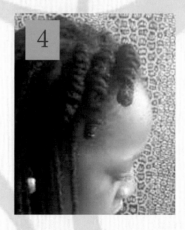

What to do!

5

- Ok so this style is really convenient for persons with medium to long hair.
- This style will make your hair appear much shorter.
- To start you take one loc of hair and fold approx 10 cms away from the scalp or ¼ the length of the loc.
- Then wrap the loc around itself starting at the scalp downward in a clockwise direction. When you arrive at the tip secure with a rubber band.
- Now this in a 2 in 1 style, you can wear loc knots for as long at you like.
- This style can provide a break from constant styling and or high tension styles.

BE CREATIVE.

Remove the rubber bands to create a whole new style, **Spiral Curlies!**

Twisted Buns

What to do!

- Similar to the sweet buns after sweeping your hair up into a pony tail.
- Hold your locs and divide into two sections. Take one section gently twist the ends while wrapping the hair around itself in a clockwise motion and secure with hair pins
- Now take the other section of hair and wrap in a anticlockwise circular motion then secure bun to scalp with hair pins.

BE CREATIVE *and combine with Maasai Bangs.*

5

SWEET BUNS

1

2

3

What to do!

- Time for some sweet buns.
- After you have pulled the hair up in a pony tail.
- Hold your locs together gently twist the ends while wrapping the hair around itself in a circular motion.
- Secure Bun to scalp with hair pins.
- You can also sweep your hair to either the right or left side to make a side bun.
- For a more creative style try a twisted bun.

BE CREATIVE *and combine with Swirly Swirl, Flower Crown or Twisted Bang. Just to name a few.*

CINNAMON ROLLS

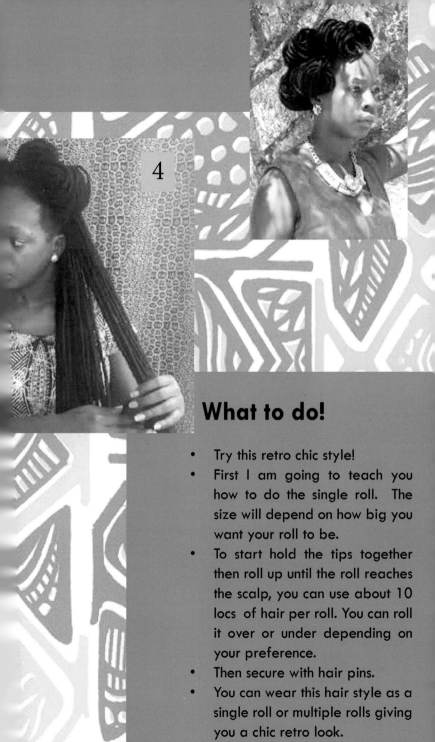

4

What to do!

- Try this retro chic style!
- First I am going to teach you how to do the single roll. The size will depend on how big you want your roll to be.
- To start hold the tips together then roll up until the roll reaches the scalp, you can use about 10 locs of hair per roll. You can roll it over or under depending on your preference.
- Then secure with hair pins.
- You can wear this hair style as a single roll or multiple rolls giving you a chic retro look.

Flower Crown

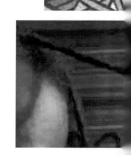

What to do!

- Let's take the Hair Flower and create a Flower Crown. Release your inner flower child.
- To get started take a few locs of hair from along the hairline.
- Take each loc and create a flower as described earlier.
- Now secure each flower to the scalp with a hair pin, thus creating a flower crown.

BE CREATIVE and combine with a Sweet Bun, Side Twist or even a Loc Knot.

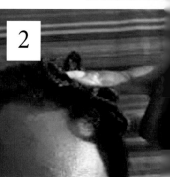

What to do!

- To start this style take a small section of hair from the temporal region on both sides.
- Separate into two sections and make a simple twist.
- Take each twist and fold to the opposite side of the head and secure with hair pins.
- Now if you have longer locs after folding the two twists to opposite sides take the ends of the twisted hair and secure at the back of the head with rubber bands.
- And now you have a Twisted Crown.

BE CREATIVE *and combine with Side Twist, Side Twist Pin Up, Sweet Bun or Twisted Bun*

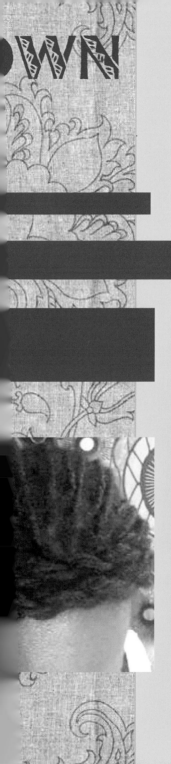

What to do!

- To start this style take a small section of hair from the temporal region on both sides.
- Separate into three sections and make a simple braid.
- Take each braid and fold to the opposite side of the head and secure with hair pins. Now if you have longer locs take the ends of the braids, wrap them around the back of the head and secure ends with rubber band.
- And you have a braided crown.

BE CREATIVE *and combine with Side Braid, Side Braid Pin Up or Sweet Bun.*

ROLL TWIST

What to do!

- This is an easy to do style with amazing results, and it's very sophisticated as well.
- So there are some variation you can try.
- First step part your hair down the middle or diagonally into halves.
- Starting at the front take about 6 locs of hair with three in each hand. Now twist the hair around itself by passing each new loc over then under.
- Continue the twisting motion by adding two-three locs each time until you reach the back of the head. Now secure by taking the loc of hair and wrapping it around the bulk of the Roll Twist.
- Repeat on the other side. After completing the Roll Twist on both sides you can take the ends of your locs and pin up into a Sweet Bun or wear it down.
- This style can be worn as a single long roll on one side or both sides.

BE CREATIVE *pin up the loose loc ends to form a Roll Twist/Sweet Bun combination.*

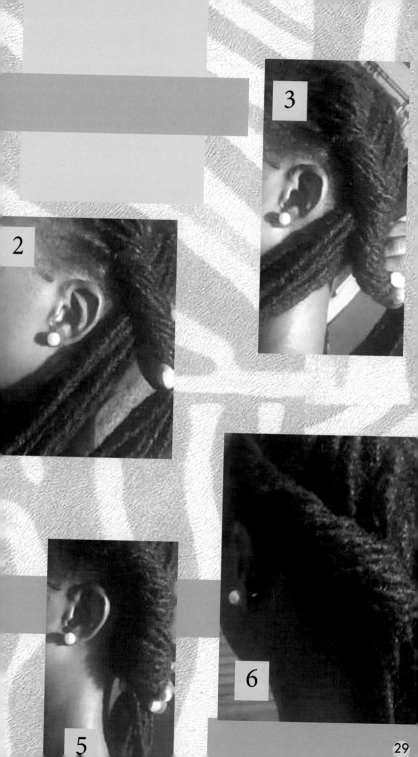

Maasai Bangs

What to do!

- I love this style. It was inspired by the Maasai Jewelry worn by the Maasai People of Kenya.
- To get started first take about 8 to 10 locs of hair from the temple region of your head (whether the right or left side).
- Now swoop the locs to the opposite side forming a semi-circle.
- Arrange the locs so that each loc lies flat on the forehead, one above the other .
- Then take the end of the locs bundle them together and secure ends to scalp with hairpins.

BE CREATIVE *and combine with a Twisted Bun, Side Braid Pin Up, or even a simple ponytail.*